WHEN PIONEERS PUSHED WEST TO OREGON

in 1843, James Nesmith and Jesse Applegate kept accurate and informative diaries of their adventures on the Oregon Trail. With the other members of the Oregon Emigration Company they trekked 2,000 miles across vast plains, trackless deserts, and jagged mountains.

Little did the settlers know what faced them as the first ox-drawn wagon rumbled out of Independence, Missouri. Ahead lay the raging Kansas River, marauding Indians, the quicksand-lined banks of the Platte River and the perilous cliffs of the Blue Mountains. Wolves, rattlesnakes, and mosquitos plagued the travelers. Clothing and shoes wore out, but still the hardy pioneers pushed westward. Old prints, engravings, and fresh color illustrations highlight the text.

This book is part of Garrard's *How They Lived* series designed to give meaning to the study of American history. Young people will find a deeper understanding and more lasting appreciation of history and geography as they see life in the past through the eyes of those who lived it.

When Pioneers Pushed West to Oregon

When Pioneers Pushed West to Oregon

BY ELIZABETH RIDER MONTGOMERY

ILLUSTRATED BY WILLIAM L. STEINEL

GARRARD PUBLISHING COMPANY
CHAMPAIGN, ILLINOIS

For Lisa Phillips

Picture credits:

The Bettmann Archive: p. 1, 5, 24–25
Culver Pictures: p. 64
Henry E. Huntington Library and Art Gallery: p. 58
Historical Pictures Service: p. 27, 91
Library of Congress: p. 18, 41
New York Public Library, Picture Collection: p. 21, 34–35, 49, 50, 52, 60, 84
The Old Print Shop: p. 2
Oregon Historical Society: p. 70, 80
Scotts Bluff National Monument: p. 17, back cover spot

Endsheets: "The Oregon Trail" by Albert Bierstadt
The Butler Institute of American Art

Contents

1. Oregon Fever 7
2. "Westward Ho!" 17
3. Dissensions and Danger 24
4. "Indians!" 31
5. The Indispensable Buffalo . . . 41
6. Trials of the Trail 49
7. Floating Wagons 56
8. The Great Decision 62
9. The Terrible Snake 72
10. Trail's End 83
    Glossary 93
    Index 94

1. Oregon Fever

Fall, 1842 to spring, 1843

Peter Burnett hauled a wooden box onto the plank sidewalk in front of Platte City's general store and climbed up on it. He looked over the crowd that had gathered in the street. It was late fall, in the year 1842.

"Friends, neighbors, and strangers," lawyer Burnett began, in his deep, pleasing voice, "I reckon you're interested in the Oregon country, or you wouldn't be here."

Burnett spoke eloquently of the glories of Oregon. His knowledge came solely from reading a book and a Congressional report, all that had been published about Oregon. "Instead of freezing winters and sweltering summers like Missouri's," Burnett said, "Oregon's weather is marvelously mild. A man can farm the year round. There's plenty of timber, pure water, abundant fish and game, and rich soil.

"They do say," Burnett continued, smiling, "that out in Oregon the pigs run around already cooked. You can cut off a slice whenever you get hungry." Everybody laughed.

Burnett told about a bill that Congress was considering. It would give each couple who went to Oregon 640 acres of free land, and 160 acres for each child.

The United States really had no right to give away land in Oregon, because the ownership of the country had not been settled. Nobody knew where Canada left off and California began. The entire Northwest was called Oregon, and both the United States and England claimed it.

Peter Burnett did not take time to explain all this. But he did point out that settlers in Oregon would strengthen the claim of the United States. "Going out to Oregon would be a mighty patriotic thing to do," he asserted. "If you'd like to join the Oregon Emigration

Company and go West next spring, step inside the store. Put your names down in my book."

Fully half the crowd followed Burnett inside the store. Among them was David T. Lenox, who owned a farm about five miles from Platte City. His sixteen-year-old son Eddie was with him.

One after another the men signed up to join the Oregon Company. Mr. Lenox signed for himself, his wife, and eight children. He wanted a big, rich farm like those Mr. Burnett had described. He would be entitled to 1,920 acres, he figured.

When Peter Burnett had finished recruiting in Platte City, he moved on to another town. Deeply in debt, Burnett hoped to make a fresh start out West, and earn enough to pay his debts. He wanted lots of company to guarantee a safe journey.

Every family that planned to go West with the Oregon Company in the spring of 1843 had a lot to do that winter. Farms had to be sold, wagons built, equipment assembled, food prepared, clothing made, and oxen trained to pull in harness.

All winter long women worked at their spinning wheels and looms. They made sturdy homespun shirts and pants for their menfolk. For themselves and their daughters, they made dresses with full, floor-length skirts. Even the tiniest girls wore long dresses and many petticoats. Women and girls needed sunbonnets, too, to keep their skin white and smooth during the long journey; no lady would allow her complexion to become tanned. Every stitch of each garment had to be made by hand, since there were no sewing machines.

There was much knitting to be done, too. Every member of a family had to have several pairs of knitted stockings. Men as well as women would need shawls to be worn around their shoulders in cold weather. Dozens of candles and large quantities of lye soap had to be made.

While the women worked at these tasks, the men prepared provisions and equipment. They dried beef, salted pork, and smoked hams and bacon. They also purchased flour, cornmeal, salt, sugar, rice, dried beans, coffee, tea, vinegar, and other staples.

On the Lenox farm at Todd's Creek, Eddie and his brothers helped their father load supplies into the two wagons that had been built for them.

"We must pack our equipment evenly," said Mr. Lenox. "We'll spread our featherbeds over it for sleeping, and we don't want lumpy beds."

When the provisions had been stowed in the wagons, Mr. Lenox put in his tools: axes, shovels, hammers, saws, chisel, spade, plow, augur, chains, ropes, grindstone, and nails. He also packed extra parts for wagons and harness, a keg of tar, and seeds to be planted out in Oregon.

When the packing was finished, Mr. Lenox looked at his eldest son. "Think you can drive the big wagon out to Oregon, Eddie?" he asked.

Eddie's eyes shone. "You mean *I'll* drive the ox teams, Pa?"

"I figure you're old enough to," Mr. Lenox replied. "At sixteen you're practically a man. I'll have my hands full herding the livestock, and Ma will be driving the light wagon with a team of mules."

Eddie surveyed the big wagon proudly. Once the emigration got under way, it would be a tiny home on wheels. Twelve wooden hoops, arching high over the wagon bed, supported a double covering of white canvas. The sides could be rolled up in the daytime and lowered at night to make a cozy sleeping room. Ma and the girls had sewed pockets inside the canvas covers. These would hold personal belongings, like slates and schoolbooks, the family Bible, toys, soap, and sewing needs. Hooks fastened to the wooden hoops would hold shawls, sunbonnets, coats, ropes, and canteens.

Eddie hung his gun from the hoops above the driver's seat, and his ammunition pouch nearby. He could hardly wait to get started.

About sixty miles south of the Lenox farm, Jesse Applegate and his brothers Charles and Lindsay were preparing for Oregon, too.

Many slave owners had moved into their county. Since the Applegates detested slavery, they decided to sell out and go to the Northwest. They sold their fertile farms and put the money into cattle, because they figured that cows would be scarce and valuable out West. The three brothers accumulated a herd of several hundred head.

Jesse Applegate, a tall, lean, tireless man, was a college graduate. He had been educated both in law and surveying, and he planned to take his books and his surveying instruments with him on the Oregon Trail. Jesse was so homely that he never looked in a mirror if he could help it, but he was honest and kind.

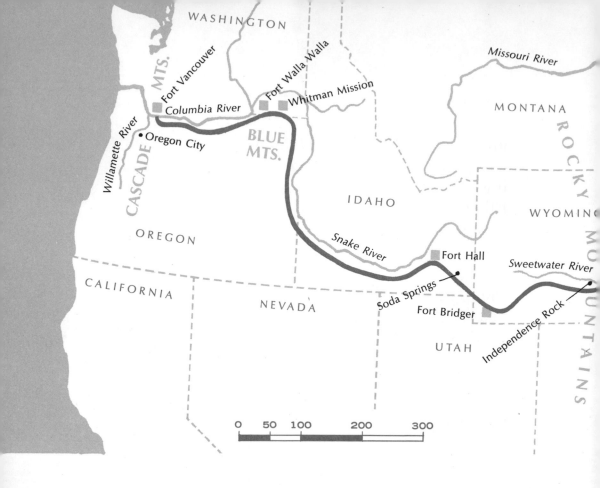

When young Will Newby, who lived in a neighboring county, heard that Jesse Applegate was emigrating to Oregon, he decided to go too. Orphaned at five, Will had had a childhood of grinding poverty, and no education. He wanted to leave the country that held unhappy memories and take his young wife to a new land where they could build a good life. Mrs. Newby's family agreed to accompany them. Like the Applegates, the Newbys bought

14

The Oregon Trail

all the cattle they could afford, and they prepared to join the Oregon Emigration Company.

With the first breath of spring, Peter Burnett stopped recruiting and returned to his home in Weston, Missouri. With the help of his sons, he loaded two big ox wagons and a small two-horse wagon. In addition to the equipment that he recommended to others, Burnett packed his law books, some notebooks for journals, and a supply of medicines for his ailing wife. He hoped that life in Oregon would improve Mrs. Burnett's health.

In the boom town of Independence, Missouri, handsome James Nesmith made his own preparations for the Oregon Trail. For a bachelor of 22, there was little to be done. Jim had no farm to sell, and no wagons or oxen to buy. He would ride horseback all the way, with his bedroll behind his saddle and his rifle in its scabbard. Saddlebags would hold his few extra clothes and the books he was continually reading to further his education. A friend's wagon would carry his provisions.

Jim had come out from Maine the previous year, intending to continue on to Oregon. But the wagon train of 1842 had already left, and it wasn't safe to travel through the wilderness alone. So Jim had spent the winter in Kansas, hiring out as a carpenter's helper. He had been one of the first to join the Oregon Company when Peter Burnett started his stump speeches.

So, early in May, 1843, the Burnetts, the Applegates, the Newbys, the Lenoxes, James Nesmith, and all the rest who had signed up for Oregon, left their homes. They began to gather at the appointed meeting place near Independence.

2. "Westward Ho!"

May, 1843; western Missouri

The muddy streets of Independence teemed with people, horses, mules, cattle, and dogs. For years the town had been headquarters for Santa Fe traders. Now it was also the jumping-off place for wagon trains heading for Oregon, because it was the westernmost town in the westernmost state of the United States.

Emigrants and traders purchasing supplies crowded the stores that bordered all four sides of the courthouse square. Blacksmith shops rang with the clang of hammer on metal, as horses were shod and wagons repaired. Saloons overflowed with shouting men bent on having a final fling before taking off for the wilderness.

Some members of the Oregon Company stopped in Independence for supplies or repairs. Others went on through town to the spring, where they filled their water kegs and canteens. They all assembled at Fitzhugh's Mill, twelve miles away.

Overnight a tent and wagon city sprang up in the fields surrounding the mill. Most of the early arrivals came from Missouri and neighboring states, but others were expected from farther away.

On May 18, after several days of waiting, the emigrants held a meeting. Speeches were made and questions asked.

Most journeys west in 1843 began in Independence.

"When are we going to start out?" asked Mr. Lenox. "They say the trip takes six months, and I want to get settled on my new farm before winter."

"Spring is late this year," Jesse Applegate pointed out. "We can't set out until there's a good stand of grass for our livestock."

"If we wait until there's enough grass for all the Applegate cattle, we'll wait forever!" retorted a farmer who had only a cow and two mules.

"Can we take our wagons all the way to Oregon?" asked Will Newby. Nobody knew. Peter Burnett's books about Oregon had been indefinite on that point.

"There's somebody in Independence right now," said James Nesmith, "who can answer our questions. Dr. Marcus Whitman has been over the Oregon Trail twice each way, and he knows all about it."

The Company appointed a committee to call on Dr. Whitman and get information about the trip to Oregon. Another committee was appointed to inspect all the wagons, to be sure they were fit for the trail. A third committee was instructed to draw up rules and regulations for the government of the wagon train.

Jim Nesmith accompanied the committee that called on Dr. Whitman. The doctor had gone out to Oregon as a medical missionary seven years earlier. His wife Narcissa was there now. Dr. Whitman had made the long, hard trip East on business concerning his mission, and was nearly ready to return.

Dr. Whitman was a handsome man, except for mottled scars from frostbite. His clothes seemed odd to emigrants who wore the customary homespun pants and shirts. The doctor dressed like a mountain man, in buckskin breeches and shirt, fur leggings, and boot moccasins. He had his motherless nephew with him, thirteen-year-old Perrin Whitman.

In reply to the committee's questions, Dr. Whitman said, "My wife and I took a small two-wheeled cart clear to the Walla Walla River. Surely, then, you people can take your wagons all the way. Your big company has a lot of strong men to make roads where there are none."

The committee members looked at each other, smiling with relief. This was cheering news.

On Saturday, May 20, another meeting was held, and the committees reported. A mountain man, John Gantt, was hired as guide, or pilot.

Cooking over an open fire and sleeping in a tent were at first a great adventure for emigrant children.

He would join the caravan somewhere on the trail. Everything seemed to be in readiness, so the company decided to leave as soon as the Sabbath was over.

On Monday, May 22, 1843, the Oregon Emigration Company started on its historic trip. Everybody was in high spirits. The children—the eight Lenoxes, the six Burnetts, the entire tribe of Applegate cousins, including Jesse's ten-year-old son Edward and Lindsay's son Warren—all believed that the journey would be one long, delightful picnic. Even Jim Nesmith expected it to be pure fun.

The company traveled fifteen miles the first day. That night they camped at Elm Grove. After supper the young people staged a square dance with a grassy meadow for their dance floor. Fiddles and banjos supplied the music. Popular Jim Nesmith danced with all the pretty girls and had a wonderful time. Eddie Lenox didn't know how to dance and, besides, he was too shy to ask a girl to dance with him. He sat in the shadows watching, while his little brothers, Washington, Davy, and Sammy, ran and played with the other boys.

Peter Burnett, Jesse Applegate, Will Newby, and other men sat in little groups around campfires and talked until late. They made plans for the trip and speculated about what might lie ahead. The women called their children in. They put small children to bed in the wagons, and older children in tents.

At last the musicians stopped, the dancers dispersed, and the groups of men broke up. The great camp settled down for the night. Nothing was heard except frogs croaking, dogs barking, mules braying, and cattle lowing. The Oregon Emigration Company was on its way.

3. Dissensions and Danger

Late May, 1843; eastern Kansas

For two days the wagon train snaked its way across the prairie at the oxen's sluggish pace of two miles an hour. Eddie Lenox soon learned that he could not hurry his ox teams, but they were dependable and obedient. He was proud to be doing a man's work.

Jim Nesmith and other horsemen raced up and down the long column of wagons and cattle, showing off for the benefit of pretty

girls. Children got tired of sitting in the
wagons and jumped down to run and play.
They played tag around and between the plod-
ding ox teams, running until they were ready
to drop. Barking dogs roamed everywhere,
snapping at the unhappy cattle.

As evening approached, some of the men
raced to be first to reach camp, so they could
secure the best camping spots. There were fist-
fights over campsites and woodpiles, hot arguments over the behavior of children, and violent
quarrels over the slowness of the great herds
of cattle.

When camps had been set up, most women
cooked as lavishly as they had done at home,

and invited friends and neighbors to eat with them. Spoiled children threw away bacon rinds and crusts of bread. They refused to eat vegetables and balked at drinking milk. Women tossed left-over biscuits to the dogs.

Jesse Applegate shook his head as he observed these things.

"People just don't seem to realize," he said to Peter Burnett, "that the food they've got in their wagons is all they're going to have until we reach buffalo country."

Peter Burnett nodded. "The books say there are no stores on the Oregon Trail, except a couple of trading posts way out West."

Two days out of Elm Grove, the Oregon Company reached the Wakarusa, a tributary of the Kansas River. The leaders got down and looked at the stream.

"We can't possibly cross here!" exclaimed Peter Burnett in dismay. "That bank is too steep for wagons, and it's nearly 20 feet high."

"We've got to cross," Jesse Applegate insisted. "We can't go any farther west until we do. I wish our pilot would show up. He would know what to do."

Finally the men figured out a way to get their wagons across the river. They lowered them down the steep bank with ropes, one wagon at a time. It took all day to get the Oregon Company across the Wakarusa.

On May 26 another barrier held up the wagon train: the Kansas River. There were no high banks here, but the river had risen too high for fording. The current was swift, and the river wide.

By this time John Gantt, the pilot, had joined the company. "We'll build a ferry," he announced, "using dugout canoes."

It was no simple matter to make dugouts, but two canoes were finally finished and fastened side by side. Then they were bridged

Sometimes the caravan had to wait while the pilot tried to find a shallow place to ford the river.

over with a platform of poles to make a ferry.

A wagon was then emptied and rolled onto the platform. Jim Nesmith and Will Newby swam across the river, carrying ropes that were fastened to the ferry. They pulled the shaky ferry to shore, rolled the wagon off, and then towed it back for another load.

One by one the wagons were ferried across. Then loads of supplies were taken over, and finally the women and children.

"Now we'll swim the livestock over," said John Gantt. Several men volunteered to swim beside the cattle to keep them going in the right direction. William Vaughn helped them.

Suddenly in the middle of the river Vaughn got a terrible cramp. He screamed, then disappeared. Eddie Lenox, standing on shore, saw Vaughn go down and he shouted for help.

Although Jim Nesmith had already swum the wide river several times that day, he

jumped in at once and went to Vaughn's assistance. He dived for the drowning man, brought him to the surface, and began to tow him to shore. But Vaughn panicked. He threw his arms around Jim's neck in a stranglehold.

"Let me go!" cried Jim. "Let me go and I'll save you."

Vaughn was too terrified to obey. He only clutched his rescuer more tightly. Jim was forced to dive again to loosen his choking arms.

When Jim came up once more with his burden, Vaughn was unconscious. Another man went to help Jim. Together they managed to get Vaughn to shore.

"Bring a keg!" Jim called to Eddie as they pulled the limp body out of the river. Eddie obeyed quickly. Jim laid Vaughn over the keg and then rolled him back and forth to get the water out of his lungs, while Eddie and the other man pumped his arms. But they could see no sign of life.

Just as Jim was about to give up, he saw a tiny movement of Vaughn's chest. The rescuers redoubled their efforts, and soon Vaughn returned to consciousness. He was carried to a tent and wrapped in warm blankets until he recovered.

4. "Indians!"

Early June, 1843; Kansas and Nebraska

It took the Oregon Emigration Company five days to cross the Kansas River. During that time people from every one of the 27 states in the Union joined the wagon train. The company now numbered nearly 1,000 people, about two-thirds of them children. There were twice as many men as women. The emigrants had 127 wagons and perhaps 5,000 head of cattle, horses, and mules.

When they had crossed the river, the emigrants halted to hold elections, in accordance with their rules. Everybody—men, women, and children—seated themselves on the prairie around the chairman of the rules committee.

"First we'll select a captain," the chairman announced. "He will have command of the company, and will maintain good order and discipline. All who want to run for captain, stand out there." A few men stood up. Others were urged to do so by their friends.

The candidates, who included Peter Burnett, James Nesmith, William Martin, and Jesse Applegate, turned at a signal and marched off across the prairie. The rest of the men ran to get in line behind the candidate of their choice. Soon each candidate had a tail of voters behind him. Each group shouted the name of its man as it pranced around the prairie.

In this way Peter Burnett was elected captain of the Oregon Emigration Company, and Jim Nesmith orderly sergeant. Jim would be second in command. It was his duty to organize all men and older boys for guard duty. To prepare for this, he took a notebook and began to list the names of all males over the age of sixteen.

A council of nine was also elected. They would act as a court on the trail.

Peter Burnett soon learned that it was not easy to "maintain good order and discipline." Every rule he made met with angry opposition.

"Who are you to order me around?" a grizzled farmer demanded of Burnett when he was told the woods close to camp must not be used as toilets. "I left my home in the States because the government tried to tell me what to do. I intend to behave as I please on the trail, and when I get out to Oregon, too."

Jim Nesmith also had his troubles.

"Why should I lose my sleep to stand guard over other fellows' herds?" snarled a poor man who had only a team of mules. "Let the rich cattlemen guard their own animals from the Indians."

One day, as the Oregon Emigration Company plodded west, a horseman streaked toward the wagon train from the pilot's party ahead.

"Indians!" he shouted. "Indians are coming. Pilot says to make a corral. Hurry!"

Quickly the wagons wheeled into a huge circle and formed a strong barricade. Men snatched their guns and prepared to defend their families.

A hundred naked Osage warriors soon came in sight, mounted on horses. With their heads shaved, their faces painted red and white, they were a fearsome sight. One Indian held a scalp, which he waved back and forth proudly. It looked like a war party!

A warrior rode close to the wagon corral. Women and children, hiding inside the wagons, shrank back in fear; even the men, fingering their rifles, were afraid.

"We are hungry," said the warrior clearly in English. "We have been fighting the Pawnees, and we have had nothing to eat for three suns. Give us some food."

The captain gave orders to provide food for the Indians, and the pioneers hastened to bring out whatever they could spare. Several donated cattle. The famished Indians lassoed them and killed them. Too hungry to wait for the meat to cook, they hacked off great chunks of beef and ate them raw. When the Indians had eaten their fill, they went on their way.

Nine days later the wagon train met another party of Indians. These were fine looking

Sometimes caravans met bands of hostile Indians. In this early print, emigrants beat off an attack.

Pawnees, returning from a buffalo hunt. They wore no war paint, and their heads were not shaved. In a gesture of friendship, the Pawnees gave some of their dried buffalo meat to the emigrants.

"Good," said the Indians in sign language. "Good meat."

The pioneers found the dried buffalo meat tough and tasteless. They could not understand why the Indians enjoyed it so much. Nevertheless, they thanked the Pawnees courteously before resuming their journey.

Peter Burnett tried for a week to establish his authority as captain, without success. Then he resigned, and William Martin was elected.

Still the arguments between the cattlemen and the no-cattlemen continued. Finally the Oregon Company split into two almost equal parts. Those who had more than a dozen head of cattle, including the Newbys, formed the "cow column." Jesse Applegate became their captain. The other 60 wagons stayed with Captain Martin. The Burnetts, the Lenoxes, and Jim Nesmith remained with the "light column."

Jesse Applegate proved to be an excellent leader and organizer. In spite of the great mass of contrary, slow-moving horned beasts, his "cow column" moved as fast as the "light column," and sometimes faster. Although the two sections of the wagon train had separate governing bodies, and made separate camps, John Gantt acted as pilot for both. The two columns passed and repassed each other on the trail. They traveled within supporting distance of each other, and members of both groups visited back and forth.

The Oregon Emigration Company had now adjusted to life on wheels. Stars were still shining when rifle shots awakened the camps at 4:00 A.M. The sleepy emigrants emerged from their wagons and tents and started their cooking fires.

Men and older boys rounded up their animals. They yoked their oxen and harnessed their horses and mules. Hurriedly the women cooked breakfast, while older children dressed younger ones.

By ten minutes to seven, breakfast was over and the wagons packed. Teams were attached to wagons. Big wagons used at least four oxen, sometimes six. Women and children took their places in the wagons. On the stroke of seven a bugle call gave the signal to start.

"Fall in! Fall in!" shouted the captains. Bull whips snapped. Teamsters yelled. Cattle lowed. One by one the wagons fell into line, creaking and groaning. The Oregon Company had started another day of its journey west.

John Gantt, with a few helpers, rode ahead each day and marked out the trail. Jim Nesmith usually accompanied him. Sometimes the trail markers had to cut or build a road. The good trail had run out soon after they left Missouri. The path was now merely a faint trace that sometimes disappeared entirely. But John Gantt always knew which way to go.

At noon, after five hours of travel, the wagons stopped for dinner. They drew up in a line, four abreast. Teams were not unyoked, but were turned out to graze while their owners ate their own midday meal.

At one o'clock the march resumed. Usually it continued until about six. Then, in the spot chosen for camp, a corral was made. The first team took its position after leading the others around in a large circle. Each wagon halted close to its neighbor, with its tongue angling to the center. The teams were unyoked and led out of the corral to graze. The wagons were then chained to each other, to form a stout barricade. Inside the corral, which was about 300 feet across, tents were set up and cooking fires built. The small children played until they were called to supper.

Men and boys gathered wood for fires, and filled water kegs and canteens at a nearby stream. Cows were milked, livestock fed and watered. Horses were hobbled or staked to prevent them from wandering off, and to keep Indians from stealing them. Kettles were hung on pothooks over the fires. Supper was cooked and served, and the dishes cleared away.

After supper the camps rang with dancing, singing, and the happy shouts of children. At eight o'clock Jim Nesmith set his guards, which would be changed every two hours throughout the night.

"Our lives might depend on your alertness," Jim told the guards repeatedly. "We are out of the States now, in Louisiana Territory. Hostile Indians might attack us at any time."

5.　The Indispensable Buffalo

Mid-June, 1843; Nebraska

Dr. Whitman and his nephew overtook the Oregon Company in mid-June, shortly before it reached the Platte River. Both of them rode mules. They were traveling light. Besides their blankets and a change of clothing apiece, they had only a ham and a little coffee.

The emigrants were glad to have a physician in the party. Besides, Dr. Whitman had been over the trail before, and his advice would be valuable.

He also had some information for them. "Lieutenant Frémont is following us," he told the travelers, "making another government survey. He has 40 men with him, and a twelve-pound cannon."

"Good," Jesse Applegate commented. "United States soldiers on the Oregon Trail should discourage Indians from attacking us."

At first Dr. Whitman and Perrin ate at Jesse Applegate's "mess," or cooking fire. Later they took turns eating with other families of the Oregon Company. Most emigrants fed the Whitmans gladly, but some begrudged them their food. People were beginning to realize that they would soon run out of provisions if they did not find buffalo.

One day both wagon trains stopped for "nooning" along the Platte River. Suddenly a great rushing sound brought the pioneers to their feet. It sounded like a cyclone!

"Buffalo!" shouted John Gantt. "A stampede! We're right in their path."

Quickly the pilot organized the camp. Women and children crouched behind rocks. Men and older boys snatched up their guns and took shelter behind other rocks. Jim Nesmith and Eddie Lenox joined this group.

"Shoot as many buffalo as you can," Gantt directed. "When they approach, everybody yell. Noise usually makes them swerve."

Gantt and Peter Burnett rode off to meet the stampeding herd to try to change the direction of its charge.

Several thousand black, bellowing buffalo soon thundered over the prairie toward the camp. Everybody shouted wildly. The men fired, reloaded, and fired again. Startled, the herd veered. Several buffalo fell dead. The others raced on toward the river, barely missing the big campsite. Over the 20-foot bank they plunged, into the Platte River.

The wagon trains had plenty of fresh meat now. To people who had been living for weeks on beans, salt pork, biscuits, and coffee, the fresh buffalo meat was a welcome change.

When the emigrants had eaten all the fresh meat they could hold, Dr. Whitman and John Gantt urged them to dry the remainder. Although no one really liked dried buffalo meat, the pioneers complied. They made numerous scaffolds, which were like rude picture frames on legs, with many slender poles laid across them. Fires were built underneath the frames, and thin slices of meat hung over the poles to cure in the smoke. After a day of such curing, the meat could be kept indefinitely without spoiling.

Hunting parties, which usually included Jim Nesmith, now went out frequently. Jim shot many buffalo. He often saw animals that were new to him: antelope, prairie dogs, and prairie chickens, as well as jackrabbits and wild horses.

Sometimes a hunting party stayed out for days and joined the wagon trains farther out on the prairie. A few hunters strayed off and got lost. Twice Jim joined search parties to round up missing hunters.

An early traveler on the plains drew these wagon train hunters shooting the unfamiliar buffalo.

The buffalo provided fuel as well as food for the emigrants. For about 500 miles the Oregon Company followed the great Platte River, which flowed through the hot, treeless prairie. During most of this time, they found no wood whatever. Fires were made with buffalo chips— light, dry flakes of buffalo manure. These burned like charcoal, with little blaze or smoke.

During the weeks that the Oregon Company traveled through buffalo country, men, women, and children walked alongside their wagons and picked up buffalo chips. Even children as young as Sammy Lenox carried bags and did their share of fuel-gathering. By the time a halt was made for nooning or for the night, each family had to have enough buffalo chips for cooking fires, or they would eat cold meals.

Women had become frugal now about food. They no longer invited casual friends to dinner, or threw away left-over biscuits. Delicacies like dried fruits were hoarded and brought out only for special occasions.

For Sammy's fifth birthday, Mrs. Lenox made a dried apple pie. She rolled out the dough on the wagon seat and baked the pie in her Dutch oven. The heavy covered kettle was set on a bed of hot coals, and glowing coals were piled on top of the lid. From time to time Mrs. Lenox added more coals, until the pie was baked.

Most of the women made biscuits daily with saleratus, or baking soda. Butter was made by putting milk in a covered can in the morning and hanging it on the back of a wagon. The day-long jolting over ruts, deep buffalo trails, and chuckholes did the work of a churn. By evening the can would hold buttermilk and a tiny lump of butter.

Cooking on the trail tried the patience of women. Backs ached from constant stooping over stingy fires, built in narrow trenches to protect them from the wind. Eyes smarted and faces burned. Cooking utensils were so few that often a single kettle had to hold an entire meal.

Along the Platte River good water was as scarce as wood. The river water was too muddy to drink, even too muddy to wash in. The men dug wells near the bank, or they carried water from stagnant pools. People sometimes drank polluted water without knowing it, when toilet trenches were dug too close to the wells.

Often the water had wiggletails in it. Then the women insisted on boiling it before using it. They did not know it, but their fussiness probably saved the lives of their families. At that time the existence of germs was unknown. Boiling the water killed invisible germs as well as wiggletails, thus preventing much illness.

Even so, there was plenty of sickness. Nearly every evening Dr. Whitman could be seen going from wagon to wagon, treating patients for colds, fevers, and pneumonia. There were also victims of accidents with gunshot wounds and broken bones. Yet many people who had been sickly at the start of the trip, like Mrs. Burnett, seemed to thrive on the harsh living conditions of the Oregon Trail.

6. Trials of the Trail

Late June, 1843; Nebraska

One lovely day toward the end of June, as the wagons followed the long Platte River across what is now Nebraska, the sky suddenly turned dark and threatening. A brilliant flash of lightning was followed by an ominous clap of thunder. Immediately the pilot gave the signal for camp formation.

Before a corral could be completed, the wind rose to tempest fury. It shrieked around the wagons, ripping off many canvas covers. When men tried to set up tents, the wind picked

Tearing prairie winds ripped canvas off the wagons,
terrified the livestock, and made travel impossible.

them up and scattered them around the campsite like kites. Wagons that were not tied
down to strong stakes were upset by furious
gusts. Loose clothing, bedding, and camp
equipment soon filled the air. Kettles rolled
end over end across the corral. Strong men
found it difficult to stand upright against the
lashing wind.

Then came the rain. It fell suddenly, in
solid, blinding sheets, soaking through clothes,
filling up boots, running through hats as if

they were sieves, and dripping through the double canvas covers of the wagons.

Hail accompanied the deluge. Some stones were the size of hen's eggs. Thunder rumbled and crashed. Jagged streaks of lightning terrified men, women, children, and animals.

For two hours the storm continued. It made cooking utterly impossible. Everybody ate cold meals and then went to bed, wet and miserable.

The next morning the pioneers woke to a dismal prospect. Again there could be no fires. Even if there had been any dry fuel, there was no place dry enough to build a fire. Matches were so new that few had any. Families had to be content with hardtack and cold meat. Each wagon set out with wet blankets and clothing draped over its top.

The trail had turned to gluey, gummy mud. It stuck to the hoofs of the oxen and clung to the wagons' wheels. In some places mud reached to the hubs of the wheels. The poor oxen lurched and floundered in this muck. Everybody walked to lighten the loads, but the animals still found the going painfully hard.

Dr. Whitman rode back along the line of wagons. "You'll have to lighten your loads," he warned, "or else double-yoke your teams."

The wagons halted. Much equipment was discarded. Women threw away cookstoves, trunks, chests of drawers, treasured dishes, surplus tinware, and even blankets. Men discarded extra axes, shovels, chains, and heavy plows. Then the wagons rolled on.

The glaring sunshine soon turned the mud to dust, and the emigrants became "dust-eaters" again.

The wagons took turns at leading the march. Every family, except the one in the lead wagon, was enveloped in dust day after day. They smelled it. They breathed it. They ate it with their food. They wore it on their skin and on their clothes. Their lips cracked from the constant dryness. Their eyes became irritated and almost blinded by the dust. When they walked, they waded ankle-deep in dust.

Everybody got frightfully dirty. Yet bathing and laundering were difficult and at times almost impossible. Once the wagons stopped for a day beside a stream so the women could do the family laundry. Water was heated in big kettles. Few women had washtubs or washboards on which to rub the clothes. They did the laundry in large buckets set on ox yokes. The wash water was used over and over before being thrown out.

Clean clothes were spread to dry on grass, if there was any, or hung on the hoops of the wagon tops. Either way, clean garments quickly became filmed with dust.

The expedition no longer seemed like a picnic. Men did not race their horses any more. Few wasted time and energy quarreling with their neighbors.

Occasionally, however, the council was called on to settle an argument. One emigrant struck his wife, and she complained to the captain. Another man tried to get his runaway daughter back, but in the hearing it developed that she had taken refuge with another family because he had beaten her unmercifully. Men "bought" guns, mules, and saddles, and conveniently forgot to pay. Guards who fell asleep were fined or given extra duty; after a second offense a guard had to stand by helplessly and see his gun sold.

One morning young W. J. Matney complained to Captain Martin, "Old Zachary won't give me my share of grub. He hired me 'for bed and board' to drive one of his wagons to Oregon. I've been keeping my bargain. But now his grub is getting low, so he wants to get rid of me."

Captain Martin called a council meeting. Matney presented his case. Several witnesses testified for him, but nobody could be found to say a good word for Old Zachary. He had been called before the council several times before.

"Mr. Zachary can no longer be a member of the Oregon Emigration Company," the council ruled. "From now on he and his family must travel alone."

There was little evening singing or dancing any more, and not much visiting back and forth. Daily Dr. Whitman rode up and down the caravan cheering the emigrants and prodding them on.

"Travel, *travel*, TRAVEL," he repeated over and over. "Nothing else will take you to the end of your journey. Nothing is wise that does not help you along."

Mosquitoes tortured the pioneers by day, the howling of wolves frightened them by night. Yet on they went, doggedly, patiently, wearily.

7. Floating Wagons

July, 1843; Nebraska and Wyoming

During the last few days of June, the Oregon Company prepared for their first crossing of the Platte River. Jim Nesmith and other hunters had gone ahead of the wagons and killed and skinned many buffalo. They brought the hides and meat to the river.

The pioneers made "boats" to use in the crossing. Three wagon beds, with the wheels removed, were covered with buffalo hides sewed together. As the hides dried, they shrank. This made the skin coverings of the wagon beds fit tight. The skins were then smeared with tallow and ashes to make them waterproof.

On July 1, the crossing was begun. First, the women and children were taken to the other shore in the "boats." Then the men ferried supplies across.

Now it was time to transport the empty wagons. All drivers yoked up their ox teams, using double and triple teams if they had enough oxen. When all was ready, Dr. Whitman, stripped to his underwear, waded out into the river. Soon he was swimming. The ox teams followed him, pulling the empty wagons. Men on horseback were ready to goad any ox that faltered.

The mile-wide Platte River was flooded. The current was swift, and there were deep holes. But worst of all, the bed of the river was full of quicksand.

"Keep the wagons moving," John Gantt shouted. "Once the wheels stop turning, quicksand will begin to suck the wagons under."

In a little while a long line of wagons reached from one shore to the other. A few wagons turned over and disappeared in the quicksand. Fortunately no lives were lost.

Next, the livestock had to be driven across the river. Swimmers and men on horseback kept the cattle from turning back or swimming

These travelers rowed their wagons across the Platte
on a raft made of planks and eight dugout canoes.

downstream. The noise was ear-splitting. Men
yelled at the animals and at each other. Cattle
bellowed. Mules brayed. Calves bawled. Dogs
barked. Children screamed with excitement.

Jim Nesmith, Will Newby and others swam
the wide river many times in the four days
it took to cross the Platte.

The Oregon Company continued on its way
and reached Fort Laramie, a post of the
American Fur Company, on July 14. The fort
stood at the junction of the Laramie and Platte
Rivers, in what is now Wyoming. Here for
the first time the pioneers could buy additional
supplies, if they could pay the high prices.

The Laramie River, a tributary of the Platte, had to be crossed now. It was too high for fording, because of melting snows in the mountains, and it looked too swift to swim.

The men decided to make a ferry, as they had done for crossing the Kansas, and take one wagon over at a time. Two boats were obtained from the fort. Then a wagon was taken apart and the planks used to make a platform connecting the boats. Long ropes were tied to the ferry, front and back, and a light line was attached to the end of the front rope.

"Now," said the pilot, "who will swim across and take the towline to the other shore?"

The good swimmers looked at the rushing torrent. One by one they shook their heads. Even Jim Nesmith and Will Newby refused.

Suddenly Dr. Marcus Whitman pushed through the crowd, leading his mule. "Give me the towline," he cried.

John Gantt tossed him the line. The doctor mounted his mule and rode into the turbulent stream. The emigrants watched, breathless. The current caught the doctor and his mule, but the animal struggled valiantly. Finally he scrambled ashore on the opposite bank.

Dr. Whitman pulled across the heavy rope fastened to the towline. Everybody cheered.

Now a loaded wagon was rolled onto the platform. Men sat in the boats and paddled, and Dr. Whitman pulled on the rope. When the ferry reached the opposite shore, the wagon was rolled off and the ferry was pulled back for another wagon.

The crossing of the wild Laramie was thus made safely, but provisions and supplies got wet and the pioneers camped for a couple of days to dry out their belongings. The women

Still fearful of hostile Indians, the settlers made their camp inside a wagon train corral.

washed clothes, bathed in nearby creeks, and washed their long hair. They mended garments and pieced quilts.

The men repaired wagons, tightened wagon wheels, cleaned rifles, patched shoes or made moccasins, and treated their oxen's feet. Boiling tar was the standard treatment for infected cuts in the animals' feet. It seemed drastic, but it worked. The travelers realized now that before they reached Oregon, their lives might depend on their ox teams. It was absolutely essential to keep the animals' feet in good condition.

Five discouraged families started back home. Others wanted to prolong their rest, but Dr. Whitman urged them on.

8.   The Great Decision

August, 1843; Wyoming and Idaho

Through the Laramie Mountains, in what is now Wyoming, the trail was studded with sharp rocks, which wore off the hoofs of the livestock. Cactus spines and grass stubble cut their feet. Many oxen went lame in spite of hot tar applications. Some men tied protectors of buffalo hide over their oxen's hoofs, and even made leather moccasins for their dogs. Wagons broke down on the rough trail. Some were turned into two-wheeled carts; others had to be discarded entirely or used for firewood.

Frequently the emigrants saw great herds of buffalo. Occasionally the landscape would be completely black with them, but the animals usually disappeared as the wagons approached.

The Oregon Company left the Platte River at last and began to follow the Sweetwater. This clear mountain stream was a genuine delight after the muddy Platte.

When Independence Rock, one of the landmarks of the Oregon Trail, came in sight, the whole company rejoiced. Almost half of the journey had been completed!

Somebody painted an announcement on the great rock:

THE OREGON CO.

ARRIVED

JULY 26, 1843

While some girls watched admiringly, Jim Nesmith climbed 100 feet to the top of the great bare rock. With a mixture of gunpowder, tar, and buffalo grease, he painted his name, "J. W. Nesmith, from Maine." Under it he drew an anchor, and added the girls' names.

The wagons followed the Sweetwater River into the Rocky Mountains. Dr. Whitman said

Artist W. H. Jackson rode with a caravan to Oregon
and painted settlers moving along the Sweetwater.

there was no longer any danger of Indian attack. The two columns of the Oregon Company
broke up into several smaller groups in order
to find more grass, water, and fuel. Guard
duty was abandoned completely.

Meat now became scarce. The pioneers
learned to appreciate the dried buffalo meat
they had previously scorned. How glad they
were that Dr. Whitman and John Gantt had
insisted that they dry so much!

The supply of buffalo chips dwindled, and
then disappeared entirely. Now the emigrants

used sagebrush for fuel. This sharp-smelling shrub almost covered the dry, rocky ground. It made a quick, hot, smoky fire, which went out almost immediately, leaving no coals.

If sagebrush had not provided the fuel they needed, the women would have hated it for it caught at their long skirts as if it had claws. As the women and girls walked beside the wagons, the hems were literally torn off of their irreplaceable dresses.

Everyone's clothes were wearing out fast, and the journey was only half over. In the evenings, and sometimes while jolting along inside the wagons, women sewed and mended. Often they put patch on patch, with any material they could find; a single garment might flaunt three or four colors. When bonnets and hats wore out, people went bareheaded. When shoes gave out, they made moccasins, or went barefooted.

The trail through the Rockies wound around and between lofty, snow-covered peaks. Sometimes high snowbanks bordered the path. During the day, the hot sun melted butter, but the nights were cold. Water froze. People wished for the blankets they had thrown away along the Platte.

Everybody knew that the Continental Divide had to be crossed. They thought it would be a single steep hill, with the rivers running east on one side, and west on the other. To the pioneers' surprise, the ascent of the Rockies was so gradual that they had crossed the Divide before they knew it. Suddenly, the streams were flowing west.

On August 14, the first wagons reached Fort Bridger, where the travelers would rest a while. A little girl died here. Two sick men had died a few days earlier.

Fort Bridger was another trading post. The early arrivals bought out Bridger's meager stock of supplies, and nothing was left for the latecomers. After a few days, most emigrants took to the trail again, but one group of eighteen—the Chiles party, bound for California—stayed behind. They hoped to find some game to eke out their diminished store of provisions.

On August 22 many of the emigrants set up an early camp at Soda Springs near Idaho's Bear River. Tents and wagons dotted the great meadow, and people scattered to enjoy the unbelievable bounty that this luxuriant mountain meadow and its willow-bordered stream provided. Women and girls picked berries and dug wild onions. Boys fished for mountain trout. Men hunted for ducks, geese, bear, and elk. The cattle, the horses, and the hard-worked teams browsed gratefully in the thick grass.

Suddenly a frightened scream brought everybody within hearing distance back to camp.

"Indians! Indians!"

Tiny figures on horseback topped the rise above the valley. Panic nearly paralyzed the pioneers. How could they defend themselves against an Indian attack? They no longer formed corrals, or even camped close together. Worse yet, many of the men had run out of ammunition.

Hastily the men moved wagons together, in a frantic attempt to provide some protection for their families. The women built up the fires and hurried to mold bullets. Children were placed in wagons and covered with featherbeds to protect them from flying arrows.

The mounted figures came closer. The emigrants worked with increasing frenzy.

Suddenly a man began to laugh. "Those aren't Indians!" he cried. "They're American soldiers! See, they're pulling a cannon."

Jesse Applegate exclaimed, "I never was so glad to see soldiers in my whole life!" As Frémont's soldiers rode past to make camp nearby, the pioneers cheered.

On August 27, after three months of steady, gruelling travel, wagons began to roll into Fort Hall, a trading post on the Snake River in what is now southeastern Idaho. By the time the Chiles party arrived, the shelves of the trading post were empty. These emigrants had found no game at Fort Bridger, and they were angry when they learned there was nothing left to buy at Fort Hall.

Richard Grant, the manager of Fort Hall, saw pioneers repairing their wagons. "You're wasting your time," he told them. "You can't take wagons any farther west. There are no roads." He offered to buy the wagons and sell them horses for the rest of the trip.

Many emigrants did not believe Grant. "He is British," they said. "He wants to keep Americans out of Oregon so that England can get it."

Others did believe the manager, and his words dismayed them. They had come more than 1,300 miles, yet 800 miles remained. If they had to discard their wagons, how could they

possibly take sufficient food? Besides, Grant did not have nearly enough horses to mount the entire Oregon Emigration Company, much less pack their food.

The emigrants hunted up Dr. Whitman to ask his opinion. They found him reading a letter from his wife that an Indian messenger had delivered to the fort.

"No doubt Mr. Grant is sincere," the doctor said, "but I do not agree with him. You *can* take your wagons. You can build roads where they are lacking, as you have done thus far.

Fort Hall, below, was a trading post for Indians and trappers. It became a stop on the Oregon Trail.

You *must* take your wagons. Only when we have proved that wagons can make the entire trip from Independence, Missouri to Oregon will enough settlers come so that the United States can hold the West."

A few of the younger men sold their wagons, bought pack horses, and went on ahead. But most members of the Oregon Company trusted Dr. Whitman. They prepared to finish their journey as they had begun it—by wagon train.

John Gantt had agreed to pilot the Oregon Company only to Fort Hall. He parted from them here. He would take the southern fork of the trail to California with the Chiles party.

Peter Burnett and Jesse Applegate asked Dr. Whitman to serve as their pilot for the remainder of the trip. Although the doctor was anxious to hurry home, in response to his wife's plea, he agreed. The Oregon settlers took up a collection to pay him, each one putting in whatever he could spare.

Dr. Whitman and Perrin went ahead of the others in a light wagon, to make a track for the emigrants to follow. And the wagons rolled on west.

9. The Terrible Snake

September and October, 1843;
Idaho, Oregon and Washington

As Richard Grant had warned, no road existed west of Fort Hall—not even a faint trail. Through a barren, rocky wilderness, the wagons struggled on in the wake of Dr. Whitman's light wagon. Sometimes they were strung out for a hundred miles.

The rough, desolate country, full of ravines and gullies, was covered with sagebrush and hot yellow sand. Dust rose in clouds so thick that a driver could scarcely see his own teams, much less the wagon ahead of him in line.

Much of the time Dr. Whitman's "trail" wound along the very brink of the Snake River canyon. Traveling the rim of the perpendicular bluff was perilous. Several oxen fell over the cliff and were killed.

The trail was also frustrating. Under the broiling, brassy sun, the temperature rose daily to 104 degrees or even higher. In the blistering heat the patient oxen, glassy-eyed and panting, suffered from thirst. They could hear and smell the rushing river, nearly 1,000 feet below them, but they could not reach it.

Grass for the livestock had become a critical problem too. The oxen seemed to be dying from lack of food and water. Some women walked ahead of the wagons each day, gathering every blade of the sparse grass into their aprons, to feed to their starving oxen.

As long as the wagons traveled along the brink of the Snake River canyon, not a drop of water could be spared for washing dishes, clothes, faces, or hands. One day Jim Nesmith reported in his journal trailing "16 miles without wood, water, or grass."

Occasionally Dr. Whitman led the wagons down into the canyon, where they followed the bed of the river. Now there was plenty of water, but absolutely no grass for the live-stock, and no sagebrush for fires. Sometimes the trail was so narrow that the rocky bluff scraped the wagons.

The travelers had almost run out of food. Many had nothing left but a little flour, beans, sugar, and tea. Some had exhausted even these staples. Children longed for the bread crusts and bacon rinds they had thrown away at the beginning of the journey. Jesse Applegate shared his food with the needy ones. He butchered some of his cattle so hungry children could eat.

There was never any dancing, singing, or visiting in the camps now. People put all their energy into traveling one mile after another, day after weary day. The crooked, treacherous Snake seemed like a monster bent on destroying them. The journey along this terrible river was about 500 miles, and it had turned into a dreadful nightmare. Besides the perils of the trail itself, rattlesnakes, wolves, and mosquitoes menaced the travelers. The choking dust grew thicker.

Salmon Falls, which the lead wagons reached on September 8, literally saved the lives of a number of half-starved emigrants. At the falls hundreds of friendly Snake Indians were fishing with spears for the salmon that came upstream to spawn. The Indians gladly traded salmon for pins, beads, fishhooks, and old clothes. One Indian "swapped" a large salmon for a pair of old pants. He promptly cut the seat out of the pants and wore them proudly.

The hungry pioneers gorged themselves on fresh salmon. They also bought quantities of dried salmon to take with them on the trail.

From Salmon Falls on, the Snake River was one long procession of rapids and falls. The pioneers lost count of the number of times their wagons crossed the terrible Snake and its tributaries. At each crossing drivers put blocks of wood underneath their wagon beds, trying to get their loads high enough to escape the flying spray. They were never quite successful. Food and equipment always got wet. Everything had to be unpacked, dried, and repacked.

Wagons at that time did not have brakes. In descending steep banks, the men "rough-locked" their rear wheels, or chained them together. This kept them from turning and also prevented wagons from running into oxen.

In some of the Snake River crossings the men towed their wagons across the river with

long ropes. Several times they chained all the wagons together, to keep the swift current from sweeping them away. In spite of all they could do, accidents were plentiful. Wagons broke down. Others capsized. Some were lost. At one crossing a man was drowned. Would the terrible journey never end?

One day Eddie Lenox was driving as usual along the rim of the Snake River canyon. His little brother Sammy, on the seat beside him, grew restless. As the wagon began to descend into a deep ravine, the little boy stood up.

"Sit down, Sammy!" Eddie snapped. "I've told you over and over not to stand up in the wagon."

Just then a wheel hit a boulder. The wagon lurched, and over the front end-gate went Sammy, down on the trail.

Eddie's heart stood still. If the heavy wheels rolled over Sammy, they would kill him! Two children of the Oregon Company had been badly injured in such falls, including a nephew of Jesse Applegate. Six-year-old Joel Hembree had been killed.

"Whoa!" screamed Eddie. "Whoa!"

The well-trained oxen stopped short. Eddie leaped out of the wagon. Miraculously, the wheels had halted a few inches from Sammy's head. But the child was limp and white.

Eddie pulled his little brother off the trail and carried him back to his mother in the light wagon. Then Sammy began to cry, and relief flooded over Eddie. Fright made his tongue sharp.

"I told you to sit down, Sammy," he scolded. "You shan't ride with me any more today."

When he returned to his ox teams, Eddie patted them lovingly. Their prompt obedience had saved Sammy's life. That evening, after pitching his tent in scorching sand as usual, Eddie unyoked his oxen and led them down to the river. It was a mile and a half of rugged, precipitous trail. The trip took more than an hour. But Eddie felt that the faithful animals deserved a long, cool drink of water.

Toward the end of September, the month-long nightmare of the Snake ended. The Oregon Emigration Company left the terrible river behind, and crossed from Idaho into present-day Oregon.

As the emigrants descended into the beautiful Grande Ronde Valley, a friendly Cayuse Indian came to meet Dr. Whitman. He had a message from Mrs. Whitman.

"Two of my friends have scarlet fever," the doctor reported. "I must hurry ahead and try to save them." Dr. Whitman indicated the messenger. "My friend Stickus will take my place as your pilot. He is perfectly trustworthy."

Away rode the doctor on his mule, accompanied by his nephew Perrin. The emigrants looked at each other, dismayed. They were still nearly 400 miles from their goal, at the mercy of a strange Indian. Ahead lay the Blue Mountains, the Cascade Mountains, and their third great river, the mighty Columbia. It was a fearful prospect.

Stickus proved to be thoroughly dependable, as Dr. Whitman had promised. He spoke no English, but as Jim Nesmith said, "He succeeded by pantomime in taking us over the roughest wagon route I ever saw."

Tall timber and tangled underbrush covered the rugged Blue Mountains. In some places the trees, 200 feet high, grew so thick that a man couldn't be seen ten steps away. Oxen that wandered away from camp proved almost impossible to find.

Under the direction of Stickus, 40 men worked for five days cutting a road through this wilderness. Then the wagons toiled up to

An early visitor to the Whitman Mission drew this crude sketch of the missionaries' home.

the summit. The gaunt, travel-worn oxen struggled painfully during the long climb. But the travelers did not dare stop to let their half-starved animals rest, because nightly frosts and a brief snowstorm warned of the coming of winter.

Going down the other side of the Blue Mountains proved even harder than climbing up. Some grades were so steep that rough-locking was not sufficient, and trees had to be used for braking. A long chain was attached to a wagon, then snubbed around a great tree growing beside the trail. Several men, working in unison, let the chain out bit by bit, so that the wagon would descend the slope slowly.

In spite of all precautions, wagons turned over. Axles broke. Oxen were killed. But the descent of the Blue Mountains was finally accomplished, and the wagons rolled on to the Whitman Mission.

Most of the travelers were now in pitiful condition. Their faces looked like leather. They were hungry and ragged. Some were barefooted, others had rags tied around their feet. Some of the women wore lacy, frilly party dresses, because their everyday clothes had worn out.

It was mid-October. Heavy snows could be expected in the Cascade Mountains very soon, and travel would be very difficult, if not impossible. Nearly 40 emigrants decided to stay at the Whitman Mission until spring. The others continued on their way.

10. Trail's End

November, 1843; Oregon

Jim Nesmith and three friends bought pack-horses for their supplies and proceeded on horseback. In some places their trail went along the steep and almost perpendicular side of a bluff that rose 100 feet above the mighty river. Brave as he was, Jim shrank from looking down. A single misstep by his horse, and both of them would plunge down the awful preci-pice to be buried in the gulf below.

Nine days later the young men reached The Dalles, a stupendous waterfall in a tremendous gorge. Here the Columbia cut a gash in the Cascade Mountains, and the great river raced

Oregon City was only a small cluster of cabins on
the Willamette River when Jim arrived there.

through the narrow chasm in a wild, roaring
torrent. Jim and his friends traded their horses
for canoes, and continued down the river by
boat. A week later they arrived at Fort
Vancouver. They went on to Oregon City, across
the river, where Jim soon got a job.

The Lenox family traded five worn-out oxen
for two fresh ones at the Whitman Mission,
and continued their journey by wagon train as
far as The Dalles. Here they learned that there
was no wagon road over the Cascades, and no
possibility of making one this late in the sea-
son. They sold their wagons, and Eddie and

84

a hired teamster were given the task of driving the livestock over the mountains into the Willamette Valley. The rest of the family hired boats and sailed down the river.

Eddie was proud to be entrusted with the responsibility of the animals, and glad to be riding horseback for a change. But he soon learned that his new job was every bit as demanding and wearisome as driving the ox teams had been. He had to keep constant guard against Indians stealing his horses and mules. Food ran low, but he didn't dare take time out to hunt, for snow flurries forecast the approach of winter.

When the trail on the south side of the river ran out, Eddie hired an Indian with a dugout to tow his animals to the other shore, two at a time. Then on they went, on the north side of the great river. Sometimes there was no trail at all, but the sound of the roaring river guided them. Eddie knew he could not get lost as long as he could hear the river.

It took Eddie and his helper almost four weeks to drive the livestock from The Dalles to the Willamette. Then on November 26 he rejoined his family in Oregon City and helped his father choose their big new farm.

Meanwhile, at Fort Walla Walla, near the Whitman Mission, Peter Burnett had disposed of his three wagons and his few animals. He bought a big boat and hired an experienced Indian pilot. The trip down the Columbia was perilous. Several times Burnett wondered how their craft could escape being wrecked on huge rocks submerged in the turbulent rapids, but somehow they reached Fort Vancouver safely and went on to the Willamette Valley near Oregon City.

When Jesse Applegate and his brothers arrived at Fort Walla Walla, they made arrangements to leave their great herds of cattle there for the winter. No boats were available, so the Applegate families sawed logs into planks and built two big boats.

As the homemade boats set out on the wide river, it seemed to ten-year-old Edward and his cousin Warren that the trip to Vancouver would be a joy ride. Glad to be free of the confines of wagon travel, the boys sat in their boat, laughing happily at everything and nothing. They laughed especially hard at their Indian pilot, at the red handkerchief he wore around his head, at his long black hair, at his breechcloth, and at his unsmiling stare.

The current strengthened, and the trip became exciting rather than amusing. Time and again the boat seemed certain to crash into a great rock. The impassive Indian would turn the clumsy craft at the last possible moment. It would veer just enough to slide safely past the rock.

Soon the current was propelling the boats downstream at the speed of a racehorse, between high bluffs that guarded both sides of the river. Edward and Warren stopped laughing. In these foaming rapids and terrifying whirlpools, even the expert Indian pilots could not manage the awkward homemade boats. Suddenly one boat leaped out of the water. Edward, Warren, another boy, and three men were tossed into the angry waves. Quickly the boat sank out of sight.

One boy and two of the men were saved, but Edward, Warren, and a seventy-year-old man were never found. The grief-stricken Applegates continued their journey down the implacable river.

Like Jesse Applegate and Peter Burnett, Will Newby left his cattle at Walla Walla. He bought canoes from some Indians and set out down the Columbia. Halfway down the river, his canoe struck a hidden rock, and Will and his young wife were thrown out. For hours the Newbys clung to the rock that had wrecked them. Half frozen by the icy torrent that washed over them and battered them unmercifully, they maintained their precarious hold. At last Mrs. Newby's family managed to make their way back upstream and rescue them.

Along with many other emigrants, the Newbys were stranded on the shore of the Columbia River gorge, near Celilo Falls. The dreary November sky drizzled rain on the famished, destitute settlers. They had neither boats in which to sail down the Columbia, nor adequate shelter, nor any food. Some desperate people boiled beef hides and tried to eat them.

What was going to become of them, Will Newby wondered? Were they going to perish, after having fought their way so close to their goal? Will looked at his delicate wife and her unhappy mother, huddling under a dripping fir tree, and reproached himself for having brought them to such a sorry state.

Suddenly Will saw a big boat moving upstream, propelled by many oars. He recognized the leader of the oarsmen as James Waters, a member of the Oregon Emigration Company.

"Ahoy!" shouted Waters. "We've brought some food!"

The boat was soon beached, and the pioneers crowded around Waters eagerly.

"Dr. John McLoughlin supplied the boat and the food," Waters explained, "and there's more on the way. Dr. McLoughlin is the manager of the British trading post at Fort Vancouver. He says you can pay him when you get money, when you harvest your first crop. He is also giving all of us, on credit, the tools and seed we need for farming."

Gratefully the emigrants accepted the food and the transportation to the coast. They promised to pay Dr. McLoughlin as soon as they could. Many of them forgot, but not Will Newby.

After almost six months of travel, the Oregon Emigration Company reached the end of the trail, in the rich farmland of the Willamette Valley, south of the Columbia River. As Dr. Whitman had foretold, the company was the means of making Oregon an American land. Their members doubled the number of American settlers in the Northwest. More important, the Oregon Company was the forerunner of many other wagon trains, because

In Oregon Territory at last, settlers began to plow the land and build homes for their families.

it had proved that wagons could be taken all the way across the continent. In a few years, 2,000,000 square miles of land came under the control of the United States.

As the years passed, many members of the Oregon Emigration Company became important citizens of the new western states. Jesse Applegate took an active part in government, and also surveyed and built several roads. Peter Burnett moved on to California and became the first governor of that state. Jim Nesmith was elected United States senator from Oregon. Will Newby started the town of McMinnville, Oregon, and became one of its leading citizens.

Dr. Whitman lived barely long enough to see the important results of the company that he had helped bring to Oregon. In 1847 he was massacred by some of the Indians he had been trying to help.

Eddie Lenox lived to be an old man. But as long as he lived, he never forgot the six months he spent driving a covered wagon 2,000 miles on the Oregon Trail.

Glossary

breechcloth: cloth used to cover the lower part of the body. It is worn by Indians

chuckholes: holes in the road made by wear and weathering

Continental Divide: the line of highest points of land on the North American continent that separates rivers flowing toward the Atlantic Ocean from rivers flowing toward the Pacific. In the United States and in Canada it is located in the Rocky Mountains

corral: a line of wagons drawn into a circle to defend a camp

dugout canoe: a canoe carved out of a log

Dutch oven: an iron kettle with a tight cover, used for baking over a fire

emigrants: people who leave one country or region to settle in another

gully: a small valley worn away by running water

hardtack: unraised bread, made in the form of hard biscuits

hobble: to tie two legs of a horse together to keep him from moving

hogshead: a large barrel

"nooning": stopping at midday for food or rest

precipitous: steep

provisions: a stock of food

ravine: a depression in the land worn away by running water. It is larger than a gully

saleratus: baking soda used in place of yeast for baking

stump speech: a speech made to the public in support of a cause

yoke: to join a pair of oxen together with a wooden frame fitted around their necks

Index

A

American Fur Company, 58
Animals
  buffalo, 41 (pic), 42–46, 45 (pic), 56, 63
  care of, 61, 62
  cattle, 13, 15, 19, 23, 25, 29, 31, 33, 35, 36, 37, 39, 40, 57–58, 62, 67, 73, 74, 78, 85, 86
  horses, 31, 37, 53, 68, 71, 83, 85
  mules, 23, 31, 37, 58, 59, 79
  oxen, 17 (pic), 24, 25, 37, 51, 57, 61, 62, 67, 73, 77, 78, 79, 80, 84, 85
  wild, 45, 67, 74
Applegate, Charles, 13, 16, 21
Applegate, Edward, 16, 21, 86, 88
Applegate, Jesse, 13, 14, 16, 19, 21, 23, 26, 32, 36, 42, 68, 71, 74, 86, 88, 92
Applegate, Lindsay, 13, 16, 21
Applegate, Warren, 16, 21, 86, 88

B

Boats, 56–57, 59, 85, 86, 88, 89, 90
Burnett, Peter, 7–9, 15–16, 19, 21, 23, 26, 32, 33, 36, 44, 71, 86, 88, 92
Burnett, Mrs. Peter, 16, 21, 36, 48

C

Canoes, 27–28, 88–89
Celilo Falls, 89
Chiles party, 66, 68, 71
Clothing, 9–10, 20, 61, 65, 81
  care of, 53, 60–61
Continental Divide, 66

D

Dalles, The, 83, 85

E

Elm Grove, 23, 26
Equipment, 61, 75

F

Ferries, 27–28, 59–60
Fitzhugh's Mill, 18
Food
  buffalo meat, 36, 42, 45, 56, 64
  fish, 67, 75
  preparation of, 21 (pic), 25–26, 37, 39–40, 42, 44, 46–47, 51, 64, 67, 89
  provisions, 9–10, 44, 66, 74
  search for, 45, 66, 67, 74, 75
  shortage of, 42, 64, 73–74, 85, 89
  waste of, 26
Frémont, John Charles, Lt., 41, 68
Fuel, 40, 46, 51, 64–65, 74

G

Gantt, John, 20, 27, 29, 37, 39, 42, 44, 57, 59, 64, 71
Grande Ronde Valley, 78
Grant, Richard, 68, 70, 72

H

Hembree, Joel, 77
Household equipment, 10, 12–13, 15–16, 52

I

Independence, Mo., 16–19, 18 (pic)
Independence Rock, 63
Indians, 34–35 (pic)
  Cayuse, 78, 79, 86, 88, 92
  Osage, 33–35
  Pawnee, 34, 35–36
  Snake, 75

L

Lenox, David T., 9, 12, 16, 19, 21, 36, 84, 85
Lenox, Mrs. David T., 21, 36, 46–47, 84, 85
Lenox, Davy, 21, 23, 36, 84
Lenox, Eddie, 9–13, 16, 21, 23, 24, 29, 30, 36, 42, 77–78, 84–85, 92
Lenox, Sammy, 21, 23, 36, 46, 77–78, 84
Lenox, Washington, 21, 23, 36, 84
Louisiana Territory, 40

94

M

McLoughlin, Dr.
John, 90
McMinnville, Oregon,
92
Martin, William, 32,
36, 54
Matney, W. J., 54
Mountains
Blue, 79–81
Cascade, 79, 81, 83,
84
Laramie, 62
Rocky, 63, 65, 66

N

Nesmith, James, 16,
19, 20–24, 28–30,
32, 33, 36, 39, 40,
42, 45, 56, 58, 59,
63, 73, 79, 83, 84,
92
Newby, Will, 14, 16,
19, 23, 28, 36, 58,
59, 88–89, 90, 92
Newby, Mrs. Will, 14,
16, 36, 89

O

Oregon, 7–8, 9–20, 23,
90, 91 (pic), 92
Oregon City, 84 (pic),
85, 86
Oregon Emigration
Company
camping, 21 (pic),
23, 25–26, 37, 40,
60 (pic), 61, 74
discarding loads, 52
disputes, 25, 54–55
entertainment, 23,
25–26, 40, 55, 74
government, 18–21,
31–33, 36–39, 54–
55
leaders, 20, 32
pilots, 20–21, 71, 79

protection, 33, 39,
40, 42, 64, 67
recruiting, 7–9, 15,
16
river crossings, 26–
31, 27 (pic), 56–
59, 58 (pic), 75–
77
roads for, 39, 79
sickness, 48
size, 31
speed of, 19, 24, 37–
39
split up, 36, 64
storms, 49–51, 50
(pic)
supplies, 9–10, 13,
15–16, 17–18, 70

P

Platte City, 7, 9

R

Rivers
Bear, 66
Columbia, 79, 83–
85, 86, 88, 89, 90
Kansas, 26, 27, 31,
59
Laramie, 58, 59, 60
Platte, 42, 44, 46,
47, 49, 56, 57–58,
59, 63
Snake, 68, 73–78
Sweetwater, 63, 64
(pic)
Wakarusa, 26–27
Walla Walla, 20

S

Salmon Falls, 74–75
Soda Springs, 66
Stickus, 79

T

Todd's Creek, 10
Trading Posts, 26

Bridger (Fort), 66,
68
Hall (Fort), 68, 71,
72
Laramie (Fort), 58
Vancouver (Fort),
86, 90
Walla Walla
(Fort), 86, 88

V

Vaughn, William, 29–
30

W

Wagon City, 18
Wagons
for cross-country
travel, 92
description, 12, 75–
77, 80–81
discarding of, 62
types, 10, 15, 20
Wagon Train (see
Oregon Emigra-
tion Company)
Water, 18, 40, 47–48,
73–74
Waters, James, 89–90
Weather, 46, 49–51,
52–53, 65, 80–81
Weston, Missouri, 15
Whitman, Dr. Mar-
cus, 19, 20, 41,
42, 44, 48, 51, 57,
59, 60, 61, 63, 64,
70, 71, 72, 73, 78,
79, 90, 92
Whitman Mission, 80
(pic), 81, 84, 86
Whitman, Narcissa,
20, 70, 71, 78
Whitman, Perrin, 20,
41, 42, 71, 79
Willamette Valley,
85, 86, 90